PAINTING
ESSENTIALS

BLACK&
DECKER ®
QUICK
STEPS ™

COWLES
Creative Publishing
A Division of Cowles Enthusiast Media, Inc.

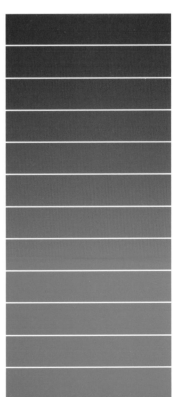

Credits

Copyright © 1996
Cowles Creative Publishing, Inc.
Formerly Cy DeCosse Incorporated
5900 Green Oak Drive
Minnetonka, Minnesota 55343
1-800-328-3895
All rights reserved
Printed in U.S.A.

COWLES
Creative Publishing
A Division of Cowles Enthusiast Media, Inc.

President/COO: Nino Tarantino
Executive V.P./Editor-in-Chief: William B. Jones

Created by: The Editors of Cowles Creative Publishing, Inc.,
in cooperation with Black & Decker. ● BLACK&DECKER is
a trademark of the Black & Decker Corporation and is
used under license.

Printed on American paper by:
 Quebecor Printing
 99 98 97 96 / 5 4 3 2 1

COWLES
Enthusiast Media
President/COO: Philip L. Penny

Books available in this series:

Wiring Essentials
Plumbing Essentials
Carpentry Essentials
Painting Essentials
Flooring Essentials
Landscape Essentials
Masonry Essentials
Door & Window Essentials
Roof System Essentials
Deck Essentials
Porch & Patio Essentials
Built-In Essentials

Contents

Repainting can transform a drab, ordinary room into a dramatic, extraordinary living space.

Interior Painting

Of all the options available for interior remodeling and redecorating, painting is one of the most cost-effective ways to create new moods and atmospheres. It's also one of the easier home redecorating options to complete yourself. Stylistically, you can exercise total creative control with your choice of colors. On these two pages, we show just a few ways in which repainting walls dramatically affects the look and feel of a room. With the wide variety of colors and finishes available, you can find a paint (or mix your own blend) to match almost any theme you desire. And you can always paint the same room again to reflect updated styles or changing needs.

Most interior painting projects can be easily undertaken by the beginning do-it-yourselfer. With the tips supplied in this book, you'll get the job done without wasting time, money or effort. These instructions show you how to paint walls, ceilings, and wood trim easily, without complicated productions or a big mess. By planning ahead and adequately preparing surfaces ahead of time, you can achieve professional results and take pride in a job well done.

Color Ranges

When selecting colors for an interior painting project, first choose a general color scheme that works with your furnishings and style tastes:

Bright colors are lively and dramatic. They create a sense of fun and can be integrated into both informal/casual and formal/traditional decorating plans.

Pastels are subdued versions of brighter colors. They generally create an informal atmosphere that works well with contemporary or country furnishings.

Earth tones create a natural feeling. They blend into the background, while providing an overall sense of warmth. They work in just about any design style.

Choosing Interior Paint

Paints are either water-base latex or alkyd-base. **Latex paint** is easy to apply and clean up, and the improved chemistry of today's latexes makes them suitable for nearly every application. Some painters feel that **alkyd paint** allows for a smoother finished surface, but local regulations may restrict the use of alkyd-base products.

Paints come in various sheens. Paint finishes range from flat to high-gloss enamels. Gloss enamels dry to a shiny finish, and are used for surfaces that will be washed often, like bathrooms, kitchens and woodwork. Flat paints are used for most wall and ceiling applications.

Always use a good primer to coat surfaces before painting. The primer bonds well to all surfaces, and provides a durable base that keeps the finish coat from cracking or peeling. Tint the primer to match the new color to avoid the need for a second coat of expensive finish paint.

How to Estimate Paint

1) Length of wall or ceiling (feet)	
2) Height of wall, or width of ceiling	×
3) Surface area	=
4) Coverage per gallon of chosen paint	÷
5) Gallons of paint needed	=

How to Select a Quality Paint

Paint coverage listed on label of quality paint should be about 400 square feet per gallon. Bargain paints (left) may require 2 or even 3 coats to cover the same area.

High washability is a feature of quality paint. The pigments in bargain paints (right) may "chalk" and wash away with mild scrubbing.

Paint Sheens

Range of sheens, from left: Gloss enamel, a highly reflective finish for areas where high washability is important. All gloss paints tend to show surface flaws. Alkyd-base enamels have highest gloss. Medium-gloss latex enamel, a highly washable surface with a slightly less reflective finish. Like gloss enamels, medium-gloss paints tend to show surface flaws. Eggshell enamel, combining soft finish with the washability of enamel. Flat latex, an all-purpose paint with a soft finish that hides surface irregularities.

7

Work light

³⁄₈'' nap roller

Paint tray

3'' paintbrush

2'' trim brush

Tapered sash brush

Painting Tools & Equipment

Most painting jobs can be done with a few quality tools. Purchase two or three premium brushes, a sturdy paint pan that can be attached to a stepladder, and one or two good rollers. With proper cleanup, these tools will last for years.

Brushes made of hog or ox bristles should be used only with alkyd-base paints. All-purpose brushes blend polyester, nylon, and sometimes animal bristles. Choose a straight-edged 3" wall brush, a 2" straight-edged trim brush, and a tapered sash brush.

How to Choose a Paintbrush

Hardwood handle

Reinforced ferrule

Spacer plugs

Flagged bristles

Chiseled end

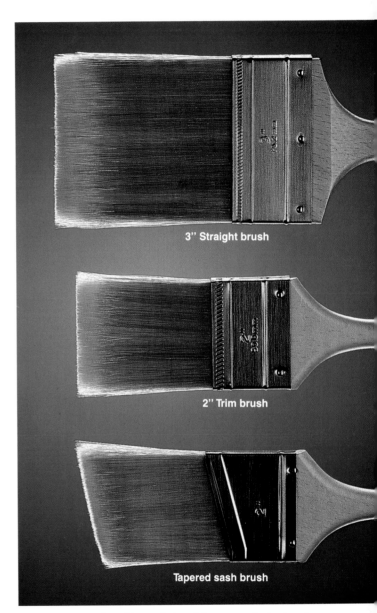

3" Straight brush

2" Trim brush

Tapered sash brush

Quality brush, shown in left cutaway, has shaped hardwood handle and a sturdy reinforced ferrule made of noncorrosive metal. Multiple spacer plugs separate bristles. Quality brush has flagged (split) bristles and a chiseled end for precise edging. A cheaper brush will have a blunt end, unflagged bristles and a cardboard spacer plug that may soften when wet.

3" straight-edged brush (top) is a good choice for cutting paint lines at ceilings and in corners. For painting woodwork, a 2" trim brush (middle) works well. Choose brushes with chiseled tips for painting in corners. A tapered sash brush (bottom) may help when painting corners on window sashes.

Choosing Rollers & Roller Accessories

A good paint roller is an inexpensive, timesaving tool that can last for years. Choose a standard 9-inch roller with a wire frame and nylon bearings. The roller should feel well balanced, and should have a handle molded to fit your hand. The handle should also have a threaded end that lets you attach an extension for painting ceilings and high walls.

Roller covers are available in a wide variety of nap lengths, but most jobs can be done with ⅜" nap. Select medium-priced **synthetic** roller covers that can be reused a few times before discarding. Bargain roller covers might shed fibers onto the painted surface, and cannot be cleaned and reused. Rinse all roller covers in solvent to prevent lint.

Use more expensive **lamb's wool** roller covers when using most alkyd-base paints. **Mohair** covers work well with gloss alkyd paints where complete smoothness is important.

Nap length. Select proper roller cover for the surface you intend to paint. ¼"-nap covers (top) are used for very flat surfaces. ⅜"-nap covers (middle) will cover the small flaws found in most flat walls and ceilings. 1"-nap covers (bottom) fill spaces in rough surfaces, like concrete blocks or stucco walls.

Cover material. Synthetic covers (left) are good with most paints, especially latexes. Wool or mohair roller covers (right) give an even finish with alkyd products. Choose better quality roller covers that do not shed lint.

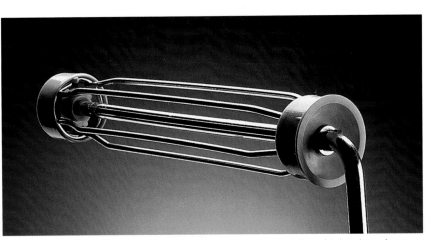

Choose sturdy roller handle with wire cage construction. Nylon bearings should roll smoothly and easily when you spin the cage. The handle end should be threaded for attaching an extension handle.

Buy paint tray with legs that allow the tray to sit steadily on the shelf of a stepladder. A good paint tray will resist flexing when it is twisted. Look for a textured ramp that keeps the roller turning easily.

Five-gallon paint container and paint screen speeds painting of large areas. Load paint roller straight from bucket, using a roller extension handle. Do not try to balance pail on stepladder shelf.

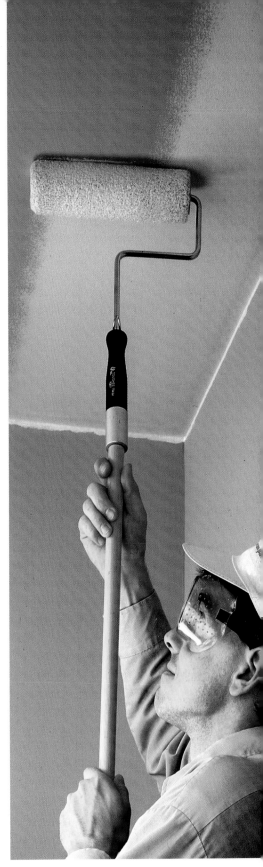

Use a 4-foot extension handle to paint ceilings and walls easily without a ladder.

Special Painting Tools

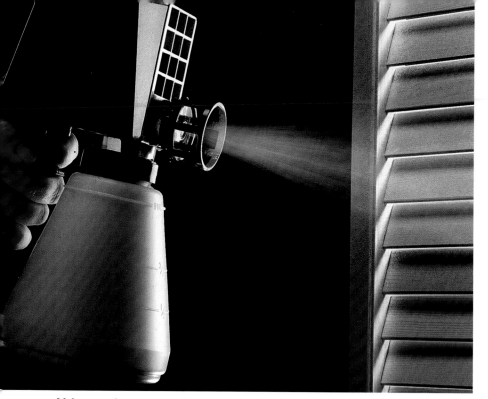

Airless paint sprayer is useful for painting large areas, or for irregular surfaces like louvered closet doors or heat registers. All sprayers produce some overspray, so wear protective gear and mask off all areas likely to be splattered. Movable workpieces should be painted outside or in your basement or garage. Thinning the paint before spraying will result in easier use of the tool and more even coverage.

Surfaces with unusual angles and contours are sometimes difficult to paint with standard rollers and brushes. Specialty tools make some painting situations easier. Disposable foam brushes, for instance, are excellent for applying an even coat of clear varnish to smooth woodwork.

Specialty rollers & pads come in various shapes for painting edges, corners, and other unique applications.

Bendable tool can be shaped to fit unusual surfaces, such as window shutters or the fins of cast-iron radiators.

Paint glove simplifies painting of pipes and other contoured surfaces, like wrought-iron.

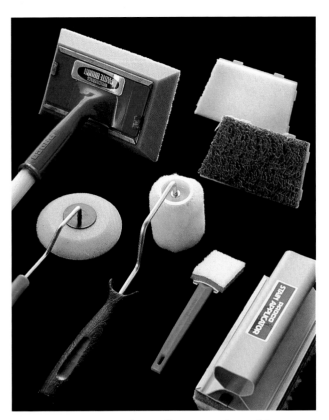

Paint pads and specialty rollers come in a wide range of sizes and shapes to fit different painting needs.

Aerosol spray paint speeds painting of any small, intricate job, like painting heat registers.

Paint mixer bit attaches to power drill to stir paints quickly and easily. Use variable-speed drill at low speed to avoid air bubbles in paint.

Interior Painting Safety

Always read and follow the label information on paint and solvent containers. Chemicals that pose a fire hazard are listed (in order of flammability) as: combustible, flammable, or extremely flammable. Use caution when using these products, and remember that the fumes are also flammable.

The warning "use with adequate ventilation" means that there should be no more vapor buildup than there would be if using the material outside. Open doors and windows, use exhaust fans and an approved safety mask if you can smell paint or solvent.

Paint chemicals do not store well. Buy just as much as is needed for the project and keep chemicals away from children. Use up excess paint by applying an extra coat or follow local guidelines regarding paint disposal.

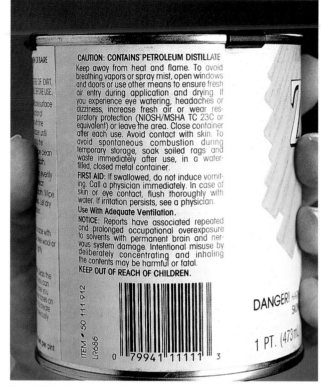

Read label information. Chemicals that are poisonous or flammable are labeled with warnings and instructions for safe handling.

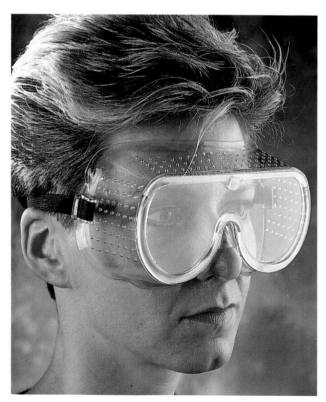

Wear safety goggles when using chemical stripper or cleaning products. Use goggles when painting overhead.

Do not use chemicals that are listed as combustible or flammable, such as paint strippers, near an open flame. Appliance pilot lights can ignite chemical vapors.

Open windows and doors and use a fan for ventilation when painting indoors. If a product label has the warning "harmful or fatal if swallowed," assume that the vapors are dangerous to breathe.

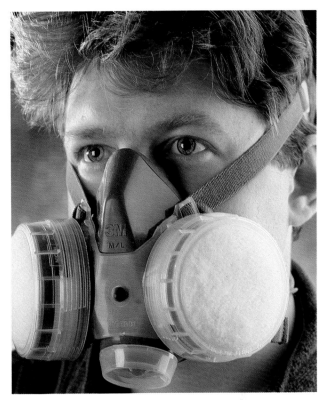

Use an approved mask to filter vapors if you cannot ventilate a work area properly. If you can smell vapors, the ventilation is not adequate.

Let thinners stand after cleaning tools. After the solid material settles out, pour off the clear thinner and save for reuse. Discard sediment.

Dispose of leftover paint safely. Let container stand uncovered until solvent evaporates, then re-cover and dispose of the container with other trash.

Using Ladders & Scaffolds Indoors

Two quality stepladders and an extension plank are all you need to paint most interior surfaces. For painting high areas, build a simple scaffold by running the plank through the steps of two stepladders. It is easy to lose your balance or step off the plank, so choose tall ladders for safety. The upper part of the ladders can help you balance, and will keep you from stepping off the ends of the plank. Buy a strong, straight 2 × 10-inch plank no more than 12 feet long, or rent a plank from a material dealer or rental outlet.

Manufacturer's sticker gives weight ratings and instructions for correct use of the ladder. Read it carefully when shopping for a ladder. Remember that you may exceed its recommended weight limits when you carry tools or materials up a ladder.

How to Use a Scaffold

For ceilings and high spots on walls, make a simple scaffold by running an extension plank through the steps of 2 stepladders. Plank should be no more than 12 feet long. Ladders should face away from one another, so that steps are to inside. Make sure the ladder braces are down and locked, and watch your footing.

How to Use a Scaffold on Stairways

For stairs run an extension plank through the step of a ladder, and place the other end on a stairway step. Make sure the ladder is steady, and check to see that the plank is level. Keep the plank close to the wall, if possible, and never overreach.

Tips for Using Ladders & Scaffolds

Rent extension planks from a paint dealer or from a rental center.

Choose straight planks without large knots or splinters. Choose 2 × 10" boards that have some spring in them: stiff, brittle wooden planks can break unexpectedly.

Push braces completely down and make certain they are locked. Legs of the ladder should be level and steady against the ground.

Do not stand on top step, top brace or on the utility shelf of a stepladder.

Center your weight on the ladder. Move the ladder often: don't overreach.

Keep steps tight by periodically checking them and tightening the braces when they need it.

Keep ladder in front of you when working. Lean your body against the ladder for balance.

Adjustable ladder adapts to many different work needs. It can be used as a straight ladder, a stepladder or as a base for scaffold planks.

Work light

Bucket & natural sponge

Drop cloth

Sprayer

Rubber gloves

Palm sander

Wet sander

Heat gun

Wallboard knives

Hand vacuum

Screw gun

Perforation tool

Paint brush

Tools & Materials for Preparation

You can reduce or eliminate most cleanup chores by buying the right prep tools. For example, buy plastic or paper throwaway pails for mixing patching plaster, taping compound or spackle. When the patcher hardens in the container, just throw it away: you'll avoid the job of washing out the pail and also avoid plugging plumbing drains with plaster.

Use a sponge or wallboard wet sander to smooth plaster or wallboard compound while it is still soft, rather than waiting until it dries and becomes hard to sand.

Buy a variety of patching tools. You will need narrow putty knives for reaching into small spaces, and a wider knife or trowel that just spans the repair area when patching holes in walls or ceilings. A patching tool that overlaps both edges of the hole will let you patch with one pass of the tool, reducing trowel marks and eliminating sanding.

Removal agents help prepare surfaces for paint and wallcovering, and speed cleanup. Clockwise from top left: wallpaper dough, cleanup solution, wallcovering remover, trisodium phosphate (TSP).

Preparation liquids, clockwise from top left: paint remover, liquid deglosser for dulling glossy surfaces prior to painting, latex bonding agent for plaster repairs.

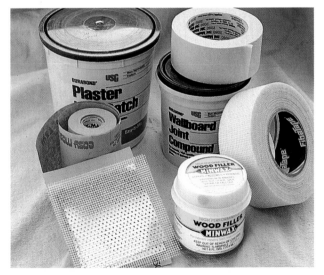

Patching and masking products, clockwise from top left: patching plaster, masking tape, premixed wallboard compound, fiberglass wallboard tape, wood patch, peel-and-stick metal patch, pregummed masking paper.

Primer & sealers provide a good base coat that bonds with paint or varnish finish. From left: sanding sealer, PVA primer, shellac, alkyd wallboard primer.

Preparing the Room

How to Prepare a Room

Before painting, your first step is to protect everything that could be splattered by paint. Remove all window and door hardware, light fixtures, and the coverplates on outlets and wall switches. Drape furniture and cover the floors. Remove heating and air conditioning duct covers. Mask off wood moldings with self-adhesive paper or masking tape.

Tip: When removing hardware, mark the pieces with masking tape for identification so that they can be replaced easily.

1 Remove all hardware, such as window handles and cabinet catches, from surfaces to be painted. If you will be installing new hardware, buy it now and drill new screw holes if needed.

2 Remove all nails, screws and picture hangers from surfaces to be painted. To prevent damage to the plaster or wallboard, use a block of wood under the head of the hammer.

3 Remove covers from heating and air-conditioning ducts to protect them from splatters. Remove thermostats, or use masking tape to protect them against paint drips.

4 Move furniture to center of room and cover with sheets of plastic. In a large room, leave an alley through center of room for access if painting the ceiling. Cover floors with 9-ounce canvas drop cloths. Canvas absorbs paint spills.

5 Turn off electricity. Remove coverplates from outlets and switches. Return cover screws to screw holes. Drop light fixtures away from electrical boxes, or remove the fixtures. Cover hanging fixtures with plastic bags.

Removing Wallcovering

Newer vinyl wallcoverings can often be peeled off by hand. Some will leave a paper and adhesive residue that is easily removed with water. With non-peelable wallcoverings, pierce the surface with a perforation tool, then apply remover solution to dissolve the adhesive.

Wallcovering remover fluids contain wetting agents that penetrate the paper and help soften the adhesive. Use a remover solution to wash away old adhesive after wallcovering is removed.

If the old wallcovering was hung over unsealed wallboard, it may be impossible to remove it without destroying the wallboard. You may be able to paint or hang new wallcovering directly over the old wallcovering, but the surface should be smooth and primed. Before painting over wallcovering, prime with alkyd wallboard primer.

1 Find a loose edge and try to strip wallcovering. Vinyls often peel away easily.

2 If wallcovering does not strip by hand, cover floor with layers of newspaper. Add wallcovering remover fluid to bucket of water, as directed by manufacturer.

3 Pierce the surface of wallcovering with perforation tool. This allows the remover solution to enter and soften the adhesive.

4 Use a sprayer, paint roller or sponge to apply remover solution. Let moisture soak into covering, according to manufacturer's directions.

5 Peel away loosened wallcovering with a 6-inch broadknife. Be careful not to damage the plaster or wallboard. Remove all backing paper.

6 Rinse adhesive residue from wall with remover solution. Rinse with clear water and let walls dry completely.

Preparing & Repairing Walls & Ceilings

Thoroughly washing, rinsing and sanding your walls before priming will guarantee a long-lasting finish. For a professional appearance, carefully check your walls for damage and repair the wallboard or plaster as needed. Pregummed fiberglass repair tapes and premixed patching compounds reduce drying time and let you patch and paint a wall the same day.

Wash and sand before repainting. Use TSP (trisodium phosphate) solution and a sponge to cut grease and to remove dirt. Wear rubber gloves, and wash walls from the bottom up with a damp sponge to avoid streaks. Rinse thoroughly with clean water. After drying, sand surfaces lightly.

How to Remove Stains

1 Apply stain remover to a clean, dry cloth, and rub lightly to remove the stain.

2 Seal all stain areas with white pigmented shellac. Pigmented shellac prevents stains from bleeding through the new paint.

Water or rust stains may indicate water damage. Check for leaking pipes and soft plaster, make needed repairs, then seal area with stain-killing sealer.

How to Remove Mildew

1 Test stains by washing with water and detergent. Mildew stains will not wash out.

2 Wearing rubber gloves and eye protection, wash the walls with bleach, which kills mildew spores.

3 After bleach treatment, wash mildew away with TSP solution, and rinse with clear water.

How to Patch Peeling Paint

1 Scrape away loose paint with a putty knife or paint scraper.

2 Apply spackle to the edges of chipped paint with a putty knife or flexible wallboard knife.

3 Sand the patch area with 150-grit production sandpaper. Patch area should feel smooth to the touch.

How to Fill Nail Holes

1 Apply lightweight spackle to the hole with a putty knife or your fingertip. This keeps repair area small so it is easy to hide with paint. Let spackle dry.

2 Sand the repair area lightly with 150-grit production sandpaper. Production paper has an open surface that does not clog. Wipe dust away with a damp sponge, then prime the spot with PVA primer.

How to Fill Shallow Dents & Holes

1 Scrape or sand away any loose plaster, peeled paint or wallboard face paper to ensure a solid base for patching.

2 Fill hole with lightweight spackle. Apply spackle with smallest wallboard knife that will span the entire hole. Let spackle dry.

3 Sand lightly with 150-grit production sandpaper.

How to Fix Popped Wallboard Nails

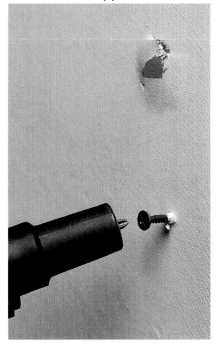

1 Drive wallboard screw 2" away from popped nail. Be sure the screw hits the stud or joist and pulls the wallboard tight against the framing.

2 Scrape away loose paint or wallboard compound. Drive the popped nail back into the framing so the head is sunk 1/32" below the surface of the wallboard. Do not set the nail with a punch.

3 Use wallboard knife to apply 3 coats of premixed wallboard compound to nail and screw holes. Allow drying time after each coat. Compound will shrink. Sand and spot-prime the patch area.

How to Repair Cracks in Plaster

1 Scrape away any texture or loose plaster around the crack. Reinforce crack with pregummed fiberglass wallboard tape.

2 Use taping knife or trowel to apply spackle or wallboard compound over tape so that tape is just concealed: if compound is too thick, it will recrack.

3 Apply a second thin coat if necessary to conceal the tape edges. Sand lightly and prime the repair area. Retexture the surface.

How to Patch Small Holes in Wallboard

1 Inspect the damaged area. If there are no cracks around the edge of the hole, just fill the hole with spackle, let dry and sand it smooth.

2 If edges are cracked, cover hole with peel-and-stick repair patch. The patch has a metal mesh center for strength, and can be cut or shaped as needed. Patches are available in several sizes.

3 Use wallboard knife to cover patch with spackle or wallboard compound. Two coats may be needed. Let patch set until nearly dry.

4 Use a damp sponge or wallboard wet sander to smooth the repair area. This eliminates dust caused by dry sanding.

How to Patch Larger Holes in Wallboard

1 Outline the damaged area with a carpenter's square. Use a wallboard saw or jig saw to cut away the damaged section.

2 Install wood or wallboard backer strips. For wood, use a wallboard screw gun and 1¼" wallboard screws to secure the strip in place.

3 Or, use wallboard backers secured by hot glue as an alternative to wood backer strips. Screw or glue wallboard patch in place over backer strips.

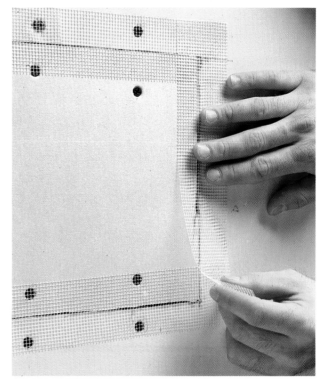

4 Apply wallboard tape to the cracks, then apply wallboard compound and sand the area (page opposite).

Repairing Holes in Plaster

Modern repair methods and materials have simplified the job of repairing holes in plaster. Coating the patch area with latex bonding liquid ensures a good bond and a tight, crack-free patch. Bonding liquid also eliminates the need to wet the plaster and lath to prevent premature drying and shrinkage. Ask your hardware dealer for a good concrete/plaster latex bonding liquid.

How to Repair Holes in Plaster

1 Sand or scrape any textured paint from the area around the hole.

2 Test with a scraper to be sure plaster is solid and tight around the damaged area. Scrape away any loose or soft plaster.

3 Apply latex bonding liquid liberally around edges of hole and over base lath to ensure crack-free bond between old and new plaster.

4 Mix patching plaster as directed by manufacturer, and use a wallboard knife or trowel to apply it to the hole. Fill shallow holes with a single coat of plaster.

5 For deeper holes, apply shallow first coat, then scratch crosshatch pattern in wet plaster. Let dry, then apply second coat of plaster. Let dry, and sand lightly.

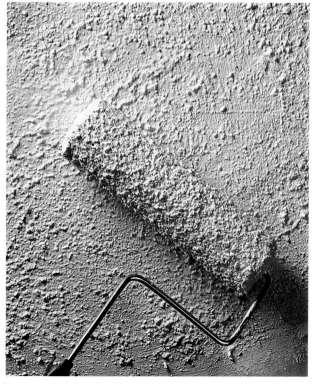

Use texture paint or wallboard compound to re-create any surface texture.

Preparing Woodwork

Before painting or refinishing, wood should be cleaned, repaired and sanded. If the old paint is heavily layered or badly chipped, it should be stripped before the wood is repainted.

If using a heat gun to strip wood, take care not to scorch the wood. Never use a heat gun after using chemical strippers: the chemical residue may be vaporized or ignited by the heat.

When using a chemical paint stripper, always wear protective clothing and safety gear, including eye protection and a respirator. Follow the label directions for safe use, and always work in a well-ventilated area.

How to Remove Paint with Chemical Stripper

1 Follow label directions for safe use of chemicals. Wear heavy rubber gloves and eye protection, use drop cloths, and open windows and doors for ventilation when using chemical strippers.

How to Remove Paint with a Heat Gun

1 Hold heat gun near wood until paint softens and just begins to blister. Overheating can make the paint gummy, and may scorch the wood. Always be careful when using a heat gun around flammable materials.

2 Remove softened paint with a scraper or putty knife. Scrapers are available in many shapes for removing paint from shaped moldings. Sand away any paint residue remaining after heat stripping.

2 Apply a liberal coat of stripper to painted wood with a paint brush or steel wool. Let it stand until paint begins to blister. Do not let stripper dry out on wood surfaces.

3 Scrape away paint with a putty knife or scraper and steel wool as soon as it softens. Rub stripped wood with denatured alcohol and new steel wool to help clean grain. Wipe wood with a wet sponge or solvent, as directed on stripper label.

Cleaning & Patching Woodwork

For the best results, woodwork should be cleaned, patched and sanded before it is repainted. A liquid deglosser helps to dull shiny surfaces so they will bond with new paint. If new hardware is to be installed, check to see if new pieces will fit old screw holes. If new screw holes must be drilled, fill the old holes with wood patch.

To renew varnished wood, clean the surfaces with mineral spirits or furniture refinisher, then patch holes with a wood patcher that is tinted to match the existing finish. Sand wood smooth, and apply one or two coats of varnish.

How to Prepare Woodwork for Painting

1 Wash woodwork with TSP solution, and rinse. Scrape away any peeling or loose paint. Badly chipped woodwork should be stripped (pages 34-35).

How to Prepare Varnished Wood for Refinishing

1 Clean woodwork with a soft cloth and odorless mineral spirits or liquid furniture refinisher.

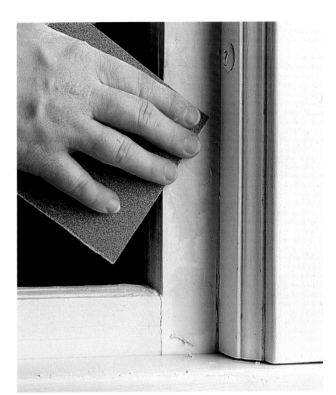

2 Use a putty knife to apply latex wood patch or spackle to any nail holes, dents, and to any other damaged areas.

3 Sand surfaces with 150-grit production paper until they are smooth to the touch. Wipe woodwork with a tack cloth before priming and painting.

2 Apply wood patch to holes and dents with putty knife. Sand patch areas lightly with 150-grit production sandpaper.

3 Restain the patch areas to match surrounding wood. Apply 1 or 2 coats of varnish (page 50).

Masking & Draping

For fast, mess-free painting, shield any surfaces that could get splattered. If painting only the ceiling, drape the walls and woodwork to prevent splatters. When painting walls, mask the baseboards and the window and door casings.

Remove lightweight furniture, and move heavier pieces to the center of the room and cover with plastic. Cover the floors with 9-ounce canvas drop cloths that will absorb paint splatters.

Masking & draping materials, clockwise from top left: plastic and canvas drop cloths, self-adhesive plastic, masking tape, pregummed masking papers. Plastic-paper laminates are also available.

How to Drape Walls

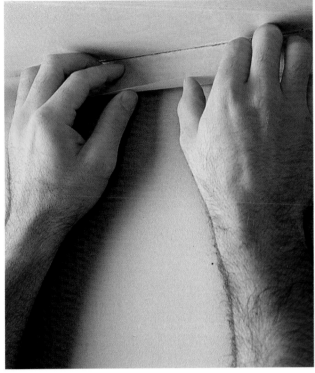 

1 Press top half of 2'' masking tape along ceiling-wall corners. Leave bottom half of tape loose.

2 Hang sheet plastic under masking tape, draping walls and baseboards. Remove loose edge as soon as the paint is too dry to run.

How to Mask Wood Trim

1 Use pregummed paper or wide masking tape to protect wood moldings from paint splatters. Leave outside edge of masking tape loose.

2 After applying tape, run the tip of a putty knife along inside edge of tape to seal against seeping paint. Remove masking material as soon as paint is too dry to run.

Final Check & Cleanup Tips

Before painting, make a final check of the work area. Clean the room thoroughly to eliminate dust that might collect on tools and settle on wet paint. Maintain the temperature and humidity levels recommended by product labels. This will help keep paint edges wet while painting, to avoid lap marks in the finished job.

It is also important for the paint to dry within normal time limits so dirt can't settle on the finish while it is wet. When applying wallcovering, a proper work climate prevents premature drying of the adhesive, and blisters or loose edges on the wallcovering.

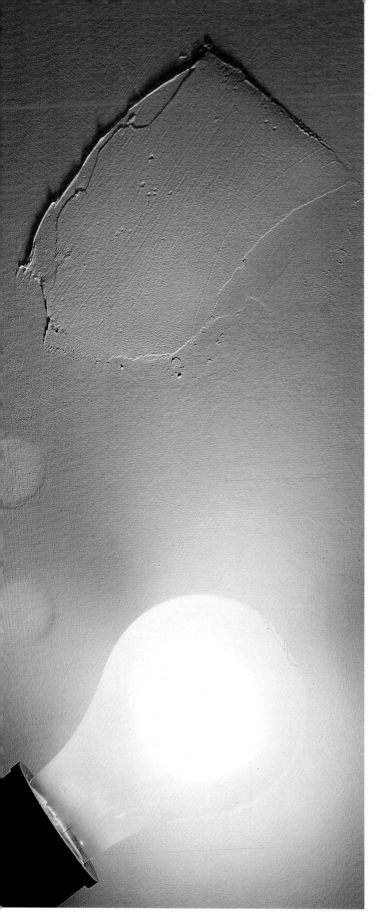

Check all surfaces to be painted with a strong sidelight. Sand, or spackle and sand, any rough spots that were missed in preparation.

Turn off thermostats for forced air furnaces and air-conditioners so that the fan will not circulate dust through the area being painted.

Sand all surfaces that will be painted with 150-grit production sandpaper. Sanding dulls the surface so it will accept new paint. Wipe walls with tack rag.

Wipe dust from woodwork with a tack rag, or with a clean cloth and liquid deglosser.

Use a vacuum cleaner to pick up the dust from windowsills and window tracks, and from baseboards and casements.

If humidity levels are low, place a humidifier in the room before painting or wallcovering. This keeps paint or adhesive from drying too fast.

Applying Primers & Sealers

Tint primer with color base available at paint dealers, or request that your dealer tint the primer. A color-matched primer provides an excellent base for finish coat paints.

A sealer should be applied to wood surfaces before they are varnished. Wood often has both hard and soft grains, as well as a highly absorbent end grain. Applying a sealer helps close the wood surface so that varnish is absorbed evenly in different types of wood grain. If the wood is not sealed, the varnish may dry to a mottled finish.

Primers are used to seal surfaces that will be painted. Wallboard seams and patch areas that have been treated with wallboard compound or patching material can absorb paint at a different rate than the surrounding areas. Joints and patch areas often show or "shadow" through the finished paint if the walls were not adequately primed.

How to Prime & Seal Before Painting

Seal raw wood by applying a primer before painting or a clear sealer before varnishing. Unsealed wood can produce a spotty finish.

Roughen gloss surfaces with fine sandpaper, then prime to provide good bonding between the new and the old paint. Primers provide "tooth" for the new coat of paint.

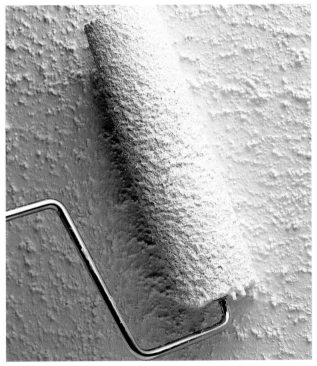

Seal textured surfaces with a PVA or alkyd primer, then apply finish coat with a long-nap roller. Textured walls and ceilings soak up a lot of paint and make it difficult to apply paint evenly.

Spot-prime minor repair areas on plaster or wallboard with PVA primer.

Mix paint together (called "boxing") in a large pail to eliminate slight color variations between cans. Stir the paint thoroughly with a wooden stick or power drill attachment. Keep paint from building up in the groove around the paint can lid. Pound several small nail holes into the groove to let paint drip back into the can.

Basic Painting Techniques

For a professional-looking paint job, paint must be spread evenly onto the work surfaces without running, dripping or lapping onto other areas. Excess paint will run on the surface and can drip onto woodwork and floors. Stretching paint too far leaves lap marks and causes incomplete coverage.

Painting with brushes and rollers is a three-step process. Paint is first applied, is next distributed evenly, and is finally smoothed out for an even finish.

How to Use a Paint Brush

1 Dip the brush, loading one-third of bristle length. Tap the bristles against the side of the can. Dipping deeper overloads the brush. Dragging the brush against the lip of the can causes the bristles to wear.

2 Cut in edges using narrow edge of brush, pressing just enough to flex the bristles. Keep an eye on the paint edge, and paint with long slow strokes. Always paint from dry area back into wet paint to avoid lap marks.

3 Brush wall corners using wide edge of brush. Paint open areas with brush or roller before brushed paint dries.

4 To paint large areas with a brush, apply paint with 2 or 3 diagonal strokes. Hold brush at about 45° angle to work surface, pressing just enough to flex bristles. Distribute paint evenly with horizontal strokes.

5 Smooth off surface by drawing brush vertically from top to bottom of painted area. Use light strokes and lift the brush from the surface at end of each stroke. This method is best for slow-drying alkyd enamels.

Using a Paint Roller

Paint surfaces in small sections, working from dry surfaces back into wet paint to avoid roller marks. If a paint job takes more than a day, cover the roller tightly with plastic wrap or store it in a bucket of water overnight to prevent paint from drying out.

1 Wet the roller cover with water (when painting with latex paint) or mineral spirits (when painting with alkyd enamel), to remove lint and prime the roller cover. Squeeze out excess solvent. Fill the paint tray reservoir. Dip roller fully into reservoir to load paint.

3 With the loaded roller, make a diagonal sweep (1) about 4' long on surface. On walls, roll upward on the first stroke to avoid spilling paint. Use slow roller strokes to avoid splattering.

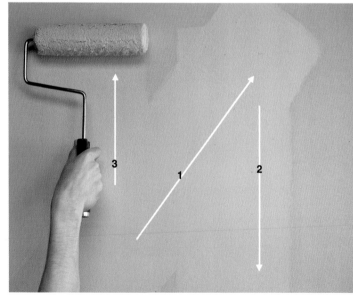

4 Draw roller straight down (2) from top of diagonal sweep. Move roller to beginning of diagonal and roll up (3) to complete unloading of roller.

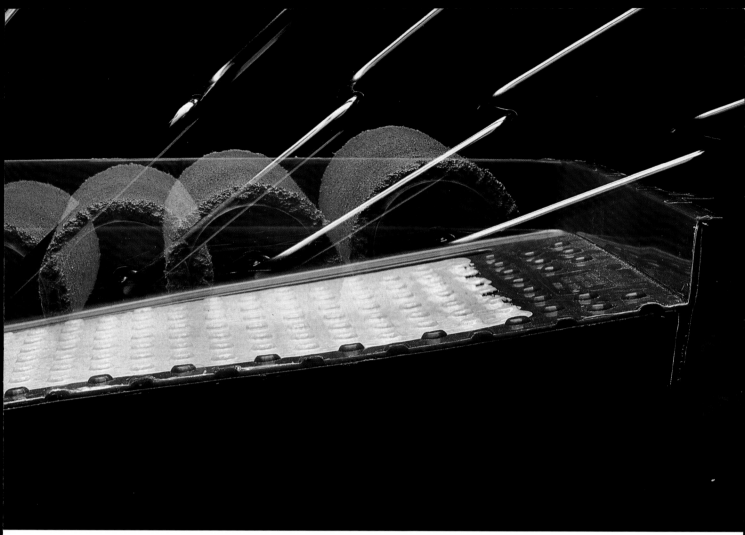

2 Lift the roller from the paint reservoir, and roll back-and-forth on the textured ramp to distribute the paint evenly on the nap. Roller should be full but not dripping when lifted from the paint pan.

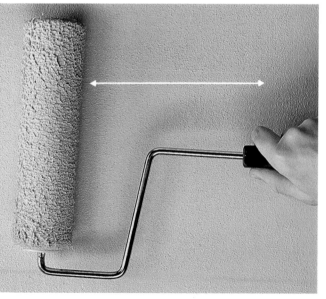

5 Distribute paint over section with horizontal back-and-forth strokes.

6 Smooth off area by lightly drawing roller vertically from top to bottom of painted area. Lift roller and return it to top of area after each stroke.

Painting Interior Trim

When painting an entire room, paint the wood trim first, then the walls. Start by painting the inside portions of trim and working out toward walls. On windows, for instance, first paint the edges close to the glass, then the surrounding face trim.

Doors should be painted quickly because of the large surface. To avoid lap marks, always paint from dry surfaces back into wet paint. On baseboards, cut in the top edge and work down to the flooring. Plastic floor guards or a wide broadknife can help shield carpet and wood flooring from paint drips.

Alkyds and latex enamels may require two coats. Always sand lightly between coats and wipe with a tack cloth so that the second coat bonds properly.

How to Paint a Window

1 To paint double-hung windows, remove them from frames, if possible. Newer, spring-mounted windows are released by pushing against the frame (arrow).

2 Drill holes and insert 2 nails into the legs of wooden stepladder, and mount the window easel-style for easy painting; or lay window flat on bench or sawhorses. Do not paint sides or bottom of sashes.

3 Using a tapered sash brush, begin by painting the wood next to the glass. Use narrow edge of brush, and overlap paint onto the glass to create a weatherseal.

4 Clean excess paint off glass with a putty knife wrapped in a clean cloth. Rewrap the knife often so that you always wipe with clean fabric. Leave 1/16" paint overlap from sash onto glass.

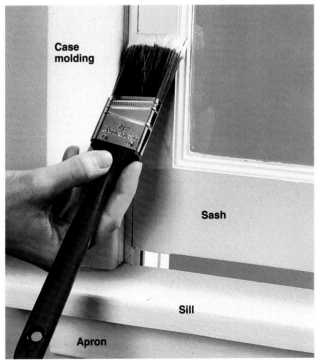

Case molding

Sash

Sill

Apron

5 Paint flat portions of sashes (1), then the case moldings (2), sill (3) and apron (4). Use slow brush strokes, and avoid getting paint between sash and frame.

6 If you must paint windows in place, move the painted windows up and down several times during the drying period to keep them from sticking. Use putty knife to avoid touching painted surface.

How to Paint Doors

1 Remove the door by driving lower hinge pin out with a screwdriver and hammer. Have a helper hold door in place. Drive out the upper hinge pin.

2 Place the door flat on sawhorses to paint. On paneled doors, paint in the following order: 1) recessed panels, 2) horizontal rails, and 3) vertical stiles.

3 Let door dry. If a second coat of paint is needed, sand lightly and wipe the door with tack cloth before repainting.

4 Seal the unpainted edges of the door with clear wood sealer to prevent moisture from entering wood. Water can cause wood to warp and swell.

Tips for Painting Trim

Protect wall and floor surfaces with a wide broadknife, or with plastic shielding tool.

Wipe paint off of broadknife or shielding tool each time it is moved.

Paint both sides of cabinet doors. This provides an even moisture seal and prevents warping.

Paint deep patterned surfaces with a stiff-bristled brush, like this stenciling brush. Use small circular strokes to penetrate recesses.

Painting Ceilings & Walls

For a smooth finish on large wall and ceiling areas, paint in small sections. First use a paintbrush to cut in the edge, then immediately roll the section before moving on. If brushed edges are left to dry before the large surfaces are rolled, visible lap marks will be left on the finished wall. Working in natural light makes it easier to spot missed areas.

Choose quality paint and tools, and work with a full brush or roller to avoid lap marks and assure full coverage. Keep roller speed slow to minimize paint splattering.

Tips for Painting Ceilings & Walls

Paint to a wet edge. Cut in edge on small section with a paintbrush just before rolling, then move on to next section. With two painters, let one cut in with a brush while the other rolls large areas.

Minimize brush marks. Slide roller cover slightly off when rolling near ceiling line or wall corners. Brushed areas dry to a different finish than rolled paint.

How to Paint Ceilings

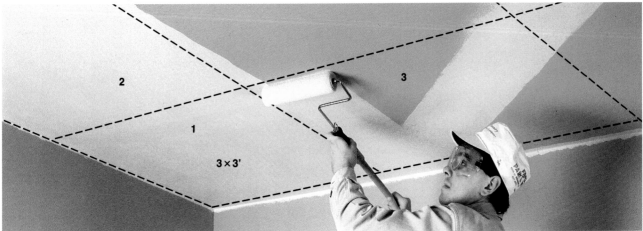

Paint ceilings with a roller handle extension. Use eye protection while painting overhead. Start at the corner farthest from the entry door. Paint the ceiling along the narrow end in 3×3' sections, cutting in the edges with a brush before rolling. Apply paint with diagonal stroke. Distribute paint evenly with back-and-forth strokes. For the final smoothing strokes, roll each section toward the entry wall, lifting the roller at the end of each sweep.

How to Paint Walls

Paint walls in 2×4' sections. Start in an upper corner, cutting in ceiling and wall corners with a brush, then rolling the section. Make initial diagonal stroke of roller from bottom of section upward, to avoid dripping paint. Distribute paint evenly with horizontal strokes, then finish with downward sweeps of the roller. Next, cut in and roll the section directly underneath. Continue with adjacent areas, cutting in and rolling top sections before bottom. All finish strokes should be rolled toward the floor.

Exterior Painting

Painting your house yourself greatly reduces the cost and, if done with care and patience, the finished product will look as good as that produced by a professional contractor.

A house-painting project breaks naturally into two stages: preparing the surfaces, and applying the paint. In most cases, the preparation work is more time-consuming than the application. But the investment of time is reflected in an even and long-lasting painted finish.

Planning and timing are critical elements in a painting project. Try to tackle only one side of your house at a time. Scraping and sanding the old paint exposes your siding to the elements, which can cause wood pores to become plugged—resulting in a poor bond with the paint. Cover the siding with primer and paint as soon as you finish the preparation.

When applied correctly over a well-prepared, primed surface, paint can last 10 years or more, especially with regular maintenance. By touching up minor problems, like chips or localized flaking, you can prevent water from building up beneath the surface. Cracks and alligatoring should be sanded, primed, and painted as soon as they occur. Left uncorrected, they invite mildew formation, leading to staining and the eventual failure of the paint. Pressure washing your siding should be the cornerstone of your annual maintenance program.

Like any project that involves the use of ladders or scaffolding, painting your house requires good safety practices. Read the section on safety (pages 56 to 59) before you start.

This section shows:
• Evaluating Painted Surfaces (pages 62 to 63)
• Tools & Materials (pages 64 to 65)
• Preparing Surfaces for Paint (pages 66 to 71)
• Applying Primer & Paint (pages 72 to 78)

Safety Warning:

Lead-based paint is a hazardous material: its handling and disposal are strictly regulated. Especially if your home was built before 1960, you should test the paint for lead using a lead-testing kit (available at building centers and paint stores). Call your local building inspector or waste management department for information on handling and disposing of lead paint.

Exterior Painting Safety

By taking common-sense precautions you can work just as safely outdoors as indoors—even though the exterior presents a few additional safety considerations.

Since many exterior repairs require you to work at heights, learning and following the basic rules of safe ladder and scaffolding use is very important (pages 58 to 59). And any time you are working outside, the weather should play a key role in just about every aspect of how you conduct your work: from the work clothes you select, to the amount of work you decide to undertake.

In addition to the information shown on the following pages, here are some important safety precautions to follow when working outdoors:

• When possible, work with a helper in case there is an emergency. If you have to work alone, inform a friend or family member so they can check on you periodically. If you own a portable telephone, keep it handy at all times.
• Never work at heights, or with tools, if you have consumed alcohol or medication.
• Do not work outdoors in stormy weather. Do not work at heights when it is windy.

Tip for Working Safely

Wear sensible clothing and protective equipment when working outdoors, including: a cap to protect against direct sunlight, eye protection when working with tools or chemicals, a particle mask when sanding, work gloves, full-length pants, and a long-sleeved shirt. A tool organizer turns a 5-gallon bucket into a safe and convenient container for transporting tools.

Set up your work site for quick disposal of waste materials. Old nails, jagged metal from flashing, and piles of old shingles all are safety hazards when left on the ground. Use a wheelbarrow to transfer waste to a dumpster or trash can immediately. NOTE: Disposal of building materials is regulated in most areas. Check with your local waste management department.

Tips for Working Safely

Permanently attach a fastener to the top of your ladder for tying off power cords or air hoses. The weight of a power cord or hose is enough to drag most power tools off the roof. Drill a hole in the ladder and secure a cap bolt (above) to the ladder with a nut and bolt. Do not tie knots in cords and hoses.

Create a storage surface for tools. A sheet of plywood on top of a pair of sawhorses keeps tools off the ground, where they are a safety hazard (and where they can become damaged by moisture). A storage surface also makes it easy to locate tools when you need them.

Stay clear of power cables. Household service cables carry 100 amps or electricity or more. If you must work near a cable, use extreme caution, and use fiberglass or wood ladders only—never use metal ladders near cables.

Use a GFCI extension cord when working outdoors. GFCIs (Ground Fault Circuit Interrupters) shut off power if a short circuit occurs (often from contact with water).

Use cordless tools whenever possible to make your work easier and safer. Power cords, even when properly secured, are a nuisance and create many hazards, including tripping and tangling.

Options for Working at Heights

Use an extension ladder for making quick repairs to gutters, fascia, and soffits, and to gain access to roofs. For larger projects, like painting walls, relying solely on ladders is inefficient and dangerous.

Use scaffolding for projects that require you to work at heights for extended periods of time, like preparing walls for paint. If you rent scaffolding, be sure to get assembly-and-use instructions from the rental center.

Tips for Using Ladders and Scaffolds

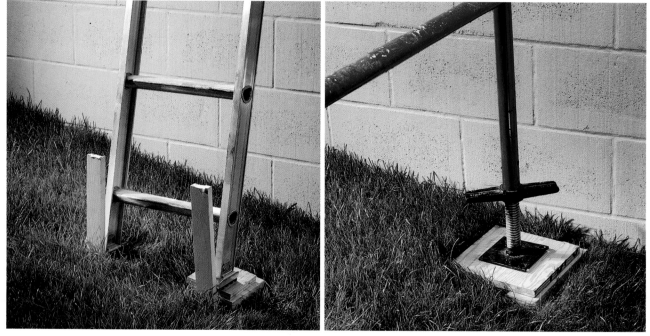

Provide level, stable footing for ladders and scaffolding. Install sturdy blocking under the legs of ladders (left) if the ground is uneven, soft, or slippery, and always drive a stake next to each ladder foot to keep the ladder from slipping away from the house.

Also insert sturdy blocking under scaffold feet (right) if the ground is soft or uneven. Add more blocking under legs in sloped areas, and use the adjustable leg posts for final leveling. If the scaffold has wheels, lock them securely with the hand brakes.

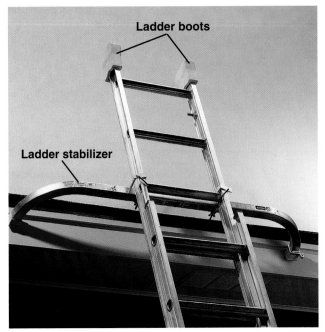

Attach an adjustable ladder stabilizer to your ladder to minimize the chance of slipping. Rest the feet of the stabilizer against broad, flat, stable surfaces only. In addition to making the ladder safer, a stabilizer allows you to work on areas directly in front of the ladder. If you do not use a stabilizer, cover the top ends of the ladder with ladder boots to prevent slipping and protect siding from scratches and dents.

Make sure fly hooks are secure before climbing an extension ladder. The open ends of the hooks should grip a rung on the lower fly extension. Use extra caution when climbing past the fly hooks as you ascend and descend the ladder, and be aware of the points at each fly extension where the doubled rungs end, and single rungs begin.

Anchor ladders and scaffolding by tying them to a secure area, like a chimney—especially if you are not using a ladder stabilizer. If no sturdy anchoring spot exists, create one by driving a #10 screw eye into the fascia. When finished with the ladder, remove the screw eye and cover the hole with caulk.

Ladder Safety Tips:

• Watch out for wires, branches, and overhangs when carrying ladders.

• Position extension ladders so the flat tops of the D-shaped rungs are facing up, parallel to the ground.

• Extend the ladder three feet above the roof edge for greater stability and to provide a gripping point when you mount or dismount the ladder (do not grip too aggressively).

• Do not exceed the work-load rating for your ladder. Limits are listed on the label of any ladder. Read all the safety recommendations.

• Climb on or off a ladder at a point as close to the ground as possible. Move steadily and keep your center of gravity low when crossing between the roof and the ladder.

• Never carry heavy items, like shingle bundles, up an extension ladder. Use a hoist (a simple cord and bucket will do), and pull the items up while you are standing securely on the roof. Lower the items down using the hoist, as well.

Using Caulk & Wood Filler

Caulk is one of the most useful materials for repairing and maintaining your house. It is used to fill gaps, cracks, and holes of every variety. It also is useful as a preventative tool—by sealing exterior seams and gaps with caulk, you keep moisture out of wall cavities and other areas that water can damage. For general exterior purposes, use siliconized acrylic or siliconized latex caulk. These products are flexible, long-lasting, paintable, water resistant, and relatively inexpensive. Use special-purpose caulks, like gutter caulk, when the need arises.

Use two-part epoxy wood fillers to patch or repair wood siding and trim. Do not use standard wood putty; it is not rated for exterior use.

Everything You Need:

Tools: caulk gun, utility knife, putty knife, chisel, brush, wooden forms.

Materials: epoxy wood filler, siliconized acrylic caulk, sandpaper, paint, stain.

Apply an even bead of caulk by squeezing the release trigger at regular intervals and moving the caulk gun at a steady pace. Practice drawing beads on scraps until you are comfortable with the technique.

Choosing Caulk & Wood-repair Products

Epoxy wood filler (A) is an excellent all-purpose product for repairing and patching wood that is exposed to the elements. Most types of epoxy wood filler come with a hardening agent that is mixed in with the product just prior to application. **Wood hardener (B)** is brushed on to damaged or rotted wood to restore strength, often before painting.

Caulking materials include: tinted exterior caulk to match siding color (A); paintable, siliconized acrylic caulk for general exterior use (B); panel adhesive, for attaching rigid insulation (C); clear, peelable acrylic caulk (D) for weatherstripping around glass; and plastic roof cement (E), for repairing and sealing around shingles, flashing, and miscellaneous areas.

How to Apply Caulk

1 Cut out any old caulk with a utility knife, and clean the surface. Cut the tip of the caulk tube at a 45° angle, using a utility knife or scissors. Puncture the seal at the top of the tube, then load the tube into your caulk gun.

2 Squeeze the trigger of the caulk gun to bring caulk to the tip of the tube, then position the tube at an upper end of the gap being caulked. Draw a continuous bead along the gap. Use caulking backer rope for cracks wider than ¼".

3 Finish drawing the bead, then release the plunger in the gun immediately, lifting the gun away from the work area. Failure to release the plunger will cause caulk to continue oozing out of the tube, creating a sticky mess.

How to Repair Wood with Wood Filler

1 Remove all damaged or rotted wood from the repair area, using a wood chisel or a utility knife. Clean away debris with a brush, then wash the repair area. For larger repair areas, attach wood forms to help shape the filler.

2 Prepare the filler for application (see manufacturer's directions), then apply it in the repair area with a putty knife (some fillers may be applied in thick layers, other should not exceed ¼"—read the product directions).

3 After the filler has dried completely, sand with 150-grit sandpaper to shape contours and create a smooth surface. Use a wood file for more extensive shaping. Paint or stain the filler to match the surrounding wood.

Evaluating Painted Surfaces

Two primary factors work against painted surfaces: moisture and age. A simple leak or a failed vapor barrier inside the house can ruin even the most carefully executed paint job. If you notice signs of paint failure, like blistering or peeling, take action to correct the problem right away. If the damage to the surface is caught in time, you may be able to correct it with just a little bit of touch-up painting.

Evaluating the painted surfaces of your house can help you identify problems with siding, trim, roofs, and moisture barriers.

Check sheltered areas first. Initial signs of paint failure in areas that receive little or no direct sunlight are a warning sign that neighboring areas may be in danger of similar paint failure.

Common Forms of Paint Failure

Blistering describes paint that bubbles on the surface. It is an early sign that more serious problems, like peeling, may be forming.

Causes: Blistering can result from poor preparation or hasty application of primer or paint. The blisters are caused by trapped moisture as it forces its way through the surface.

Solution: Scrape and touch up localized blistering. For widespread damage, remove paint down to bare wood, then apply new primer and paint.

Peeling occurs when paint disengages entirely from the surface, falling away in flakes.

Causes: Peeling is most often associated with persistent moisture problems, generally from a leak or a failed vapor barrier.

Solution: Identify and correct any moisture problems. If the peeling is localized, scrape and sand the damaged area only, then touch up with new primer and paint. If peeling is widespread, remove the old paint down to bare wood. Apply new primer and paint.

Alligatoring is widespread flaking and cracking of surfaces, typically seen on old paint and surfaces with many built-up layers of paint.

Causes: Alligatoring can be caused by excessive layers of paint, inadequate surface preparation, or insufficient drying time for a primer.

Solution: Repainting will not permanently cover significant alligatoring. Remove the old paint down to bare wood, then prime and repaint.

Detecting the Source of Moisture Beneath a Painted Surface

Localized blistering and peeling indicates that moisture, usually from a leaky roof or gutter system, is trapped under the paint. Check roofing and gutter materials to find the source of the leak. Also look for leaking pipes inside the wall. Correct the moisture problem before you repaint.

Clearly defined blistering and peeling occurs when a humid room, like a bathroom, has an insufficient vapor barrier. If there is a clear line where an interior wall ends, you probably will need to remove the wall coverings and replace the vapor barrier. In some cases, you may be able to solve the problem by increasing ventilation or adding a dehumidifier.

Identifying Common Surface Problems

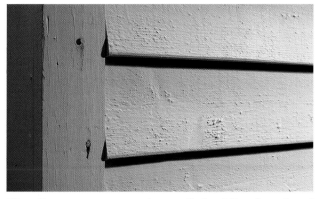

Mildew forms in cracks and in humid areas that receive little direct sunlight. Wash the areas with a 1:1 solution of household chlorine bleach and water, or with trisodium phosphate (TSP) to kill the mildew.

Rust occurs when moisture penetrates failed paint on iron or steel. Remove the rust and any loose paint with a wire brush attachment and portable drill, then prime and repaint the affected area.

Bleeding spots occur when nails in siding "pop" and turn rusty. Remove the nails, sand out the rust, and drive in new ring-shank siding nails. Apply metal primer, then paint to blend in.

Efflorescence occurs in masonry when minerals leech through the surface, forming a crystalline or powdery layer. Use muriatic acid to remove efflorescence before priming and painting.

Materials for painting include: tarps, masking tape, sandpaper, caulk, primers (tinted to match paint color), house paint, trim paint, and special-task paints.

Exterior Painting Tools & Materials

An investment in quality primer and house paint will make your hard work last for years longer than if you use cheaper products. High-quality preparation and application tools are also a good investment because they produce better results with less work.

Traditionally, almost all house paint was oil-based. But new latex-based products now rival oil-based products in durability and appearance, without the hazards, odors, and disposal problems of oil-based paints.

How to Estimate Your Paint Needs

Add:
square footage of walls (length × height)
square footage of soffit panels
15% allowance for waste
Subtract:
square footage of doors and windows

Find the coverage rate on the labels of the paint you will use (350 square feet per gallon is an average rate). Divide the total square footage by the coverage rate to determine the number of gallons you will need for each coat.

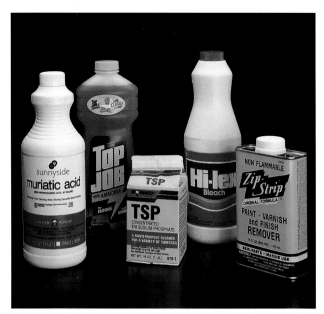

Chemicals and cleaners for paint maintenance and for surface preparation include (from left): muriatic acid for cleaning rust from metal, household detergent and TSP (trisodium phosphate) for general washing of surfaces, household chlorine bleach for cleaning mildew, and chemical stripper for removing thick layers of paint from delicate surfaces.

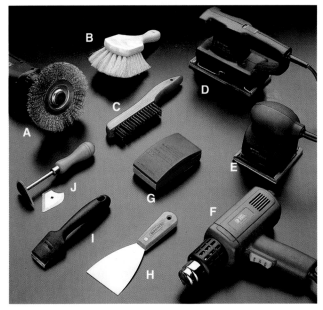

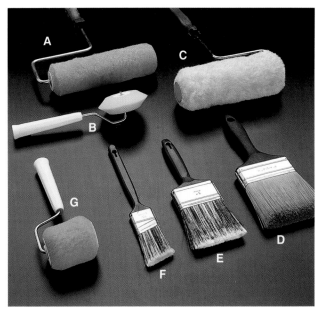

Tools for paint removal include: drill with wire-wheel attachment (A), stiff-bristled scrub brush (B), wire brush (C), ⅓-sheet finishing sander (D), ¼-sheet finishing sander (E), heat gun (F), sanding block (G), putty knife (H), paint scraper (I), and detail scraper with interchangeable heads (J).

Tools for applying paint include: roller and sleeve with ⅜" nap for smooth or semi-smooth surfaces (A), corner roller for corners and trim (B), roller with ⅝" nap for rough surfaces (C), 4" paint brush for lap siding (D), 3" paint brush for siding and trim (E), 2" sash brush for trim and window frames (F), 3"-wide roller for painting trim (G). NOTE: All brushes shown have synthetic bristles for use with latex-based paint.

Rent a pressure washer and attachments for the surface-preparation process. A pressure washer cleans siding thoroughly, and removes old, flaky paint. A nozzle with an extension pole attaches to the hose from the pressure washer. Accessories, like the rotating scrub brush shown, clean hard-to-reach areas.

Sanded to bare wood

Scraped and spot-sanded

Pressure-washed only

Preparing Surfaces for Paint

Preparing the surface is a crucial part of the house-painting process. Generally, the more preparation work you do, the smoother and more long-lasting the finished surface will be. But anyone who paints his or her house learns quickly that there is a point of diminishing return when it comes to preparation. You must decide for yourself how much sanding and scraping is enough for you to obtain a finish that meets your demands. But whether you are attempting to create a glass-smooth finish with a professional look or you simply want to freshen up the look of your house, always remove and spot-sand all paint that has lost its bond with the surface.

Preparation defines the final appearance. For the smoothest finish, sand all the way to bare wood with a power sander (top). For a less time-consuming (but rougher) finish, scrape off loose paint, then spot-sand the rough edges (middle). Pressure-washing alone removes some flaky paint, but it will not create a satisfactory finish (bottom).

Everything You Need:

Tools: pressure washer, paint scrapers, finishing sander, wire brush, stiff-bristled brush, file, sanding blocks, hammer, putty knife.

Materials: sandpaper, epoxy wood filler, caulk, colored push pins, tape.

Tips for Pressure-washing

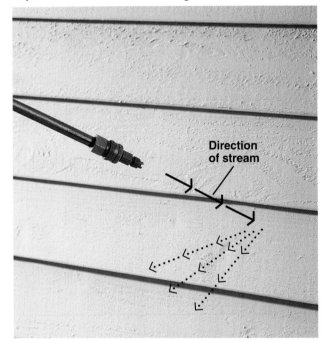

Direction of stream

Direct the water stream at a downward angle when pressure-washing siding. Avoid getting too close to the surface with the sprayer head, because the force of the stream can damage siding and trim. When pressure-washing high on the wall, use an extension attachment (page 65).

Attach a rotating scrub brush attachment to clean hard-to-reach areas, like cornices and soffits. Check with the rental store for available pressure-washer accessories.

Tips for Protecting Your House & Yard

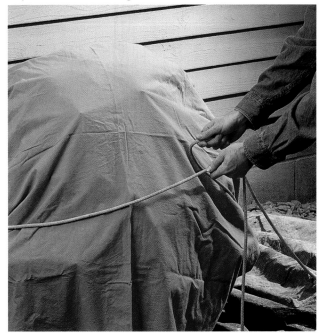

Protect delicate plants and shrubs with tarps when you are working near them. Also lay tarps on the ground around your house to collect debris. Turn off air conditioners and other appliances, and cover them with plastic sheets to protect them from debris and paint.

Remove shutters and decorative trim to protect them from damage and to give you better access to the surface of your house. Inspect the shutters and trim to see if they are in good repair, and fix them if necessary. Prepare, prime, and paint them before reinstalling.

Options for Removing Paint

Use a heat gun to loosen thick layers of paint. Aim the gun at the surface, and move it constantly. Follow with a scraper once the paint releases. Read the manufacturer's directions and precautions.

Use chemical stripper to remove paint from delicate trim. Work in a well-ventilated area, wearing heavy-duty rubber gloves. Read the stripper manufacturer's directions and precautions.

Rent a siding sander to remove large areas of paint on wood lap siding. Rent a sander with a disk the same diameter as the width of the reveal area on your siding. Get instructions from the rental store.

How to Prepare Surfaces for Paint

1 Pressure-wash your house (page 66). Pressure-washing cleans the surface and dislodges loose paint. Allow the house to dry thoroughly before continuing with the preparation work.

2 Scrape off loose paint that was not removed during pressure-washing, using a paint scraper. Be careful not to damage the surface with overly aggressive scraping.

3 Remove loose paint in hard-to-reach areas with detail scrapers (available at building centers and woodworker's stores). Some have interchangeable heads that match common trim profiles.

4 Use a finishing sander with 80-grit sandpaper to smooth out rough paint.

5 Use sanding blocks and 80 to 120-grit sandpaper to remove paint and smooth out ridges in hard-to-reach areas of trim. Sanding blocks are available at building centers in a variety of shapes and sizes, like the teardrop design shown here. Or, you can make your own blocks from dowels, wood scraps, garden hose, or other household materials.

6 Inspect all surfaces for cracks, rot, or other damage. Mark damaged areas with colored push pins or tape so you can locate them easily when making repairs.

7 Repair all the damaged areas (pages 36 to 37 and 60 to 61).

8 Use a finishing sander with 120-grit sandpaper to sand down ridges and hard edges left from the scraping process, creating a smooth surface. Also sand repaired areas.

(continued next page)

How to Prepare Surfaces for Paint (continued)

9 Scuff-sand glossy surfaces on doors, window casings, and any surfaces painted with enamel paint, using a coarse abrasive pad or 150-grit sandpaper. Scuffing creates a better bonding surface for primer and paint.

10 Fill cracks in siding and gaps around window and door trim with paintable siliconized acrylic caulk. The caulk makes a tight, long-lasting seal.

Tips for Removing Clear Finishes

Pressure-wash stained or unpainted surfaces that have been treated with a wood preservative or protectant (page 66) before recoating with fresh sealant. Clear topcoats and sealants can flake and peel, just like paint.

Use a stiff-bristled brush to dislodge any flakes of loosened surface coating not removed by pressure-washing. Do not use a wire brush on wood surfaces.

Tips for Removing Paint from Metal & Masonry

Use a wire brush to remove loose paint and rust from metal hardware, like railings and ornate trim. Cover the surface with metal primer immediately after brushing to prevent new rust from forming.

Scuff-sand metal siding and trim with medium-coarse steel wool or a coarse abrasive pad. Wash the surface before priming and painting.

Use a drill with a wire-wheel attachment to remove loose mortar, mineral deposits, or paint from mortar lines in masonry surfaces. Clean broad, flat surfaces with a wire brush. Correct any minor damage with masonry repair products.

Remove rust from metal hardware with diluted muriatic acid solution. CAUTION: When working with muriatic acid, wear safety equipment, work in a well-ventilated area, and follow the manufacturer's directions and precautions.

Paint downward from the top of your house, covering as much surface as you can reach comfortably without moving your ladder or scaffolding. After the primer or paint dries, return to each section and touch up any unpainted areas that were covered by the pads of the ladder or ladder stabilizer.

Applying Primer & Paint

Like doing preparation work, applying primer and paint requires good planning and execution. If you use a quality primer that is tinted to match the color of your house paint as closely as possible, you can often achieve good coverage with only one coat of house paint.

Keep an eye on the weather when you are planning to paint. Damp weather or rain that falls within an hour or two of application will ruin your paint job. Do not apply paint when the temperature is below 50°F, or above 90°F. And avoid working during high winds—it is unsafe, and dust and dirt are likely to blow onto the freshly painted surface.

TIP: Apply primer and paint in the shade or in indirect sunlight. Direct sunlight dries primers and paints too rapidly, causing moisture to become trapped below the dried surface. This can result in blistering, peeling, and other types of paint failure. Also, lap marks and brush marks are more likely to show up if paint is applied in direct sunlight.

Tips for Applying Primer & Paint

Use the best type of primer or paint for the job. For best results, use a metal primer with rust inhibitor for metal surfaces, and use masonry primer with an anti-chalking additive for masonry surfaces. Always read the manufacturer's recommendations for use.

Follow a logical painting sequence. For example, priming and painting wood stairs and porch floors *after* walls, doors, and trim prevents the need to touch up spills.

Options for Applying Primer & Paint

Use paint brushes for maximum control of the materials. Have clean 4" and 2½" or 3" brushes on hand, as well as a tapered sash brush (page 65). Using brushes that fit the area helps you create a professional-looking finish.

Use paint rollers to paint smooth surfaces quickly. Use a roller with an 8" or 9" roller sleeve (top) for broad surfaces. Use a 3"-wide roller to paint flat-surfaced trim, like end caps (bottom).

Use a power sprayer to apply paint to porch railings, ornate trim, shutters, and other hard-to-paint metal hardware. Read the manufacturer's directions before you start. NOTE: Professional-quality airless sprayers can be rented for large spray-painting projects.

Tips for Painting with a Paint Brush

Load your paint brush with the correct amount of paint for the area you are painting. Use a full load for broad areas, a moderate load for smaller areas and feathering strokes, and a light load when painting or working around trim.

Hold the paint brush at a 45° angle when painting broad, flat areas. Apply just enough downward pressure to flex the bristles and "squeeze" the paint out of the brush. Load your brush properly (photo, left), use good brushing technique, and avoid overbrushing to achieve smooth, pleasing results.

How to Apply Paint to Flat Surfaces

1 Load your paint brush with a full load of paint. Starting at one end of the surface, make a long, smooth stroke until the paint begins to "feather" out.

2 As you finish the stroke, lift the brush gradually from the surface so you do not leave a definite ending point. If the paint appears uneven or contains heavy brush marks, smooth it out with the brush. Be careful to avoid overbrushing.

3 Reload your brush and make another stroke from the other direction, painting over the feathered end of the first stroke to create a smooth, even surface. If the area where the two strokes meet is noticeable, rebrush it with a light load of paint. Feather out the starting point of the second stroke to avoid lap marks.

How to Apply Primer & Paint to Your House

Of all the steps involved in painting your house, applying paint is perhaps the most satisfying. Prime all surfaces to be painted, then go back and apply the paint. Allow ample drying time for primers before applying paint.

If you use quality primer that is tinted in the color range of your house paint or trim paint, you should get suffcient paint coverage with just one coat.

Everything You Need:

Tools: 4" paint brush, 2½" or 3" paint brush, sash brush, scaffolding or ladder.

Materials: primers, house paint, trim paint, cleanup materials.

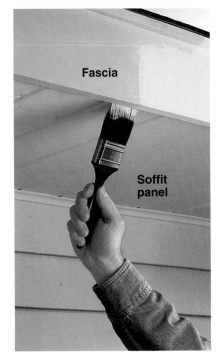

Fascia

Soffit panel

1 Paint the face of the fascia first, then cut in paint at the bottom edges of soffit panels. NOTE: Fascia and soffits are usually painted the same color as the trim.

TIP: Paint gutters and downspouts after painting the fascia, beginning with the back sides and working toward the front. If you use metal primer, you can paint gutters and downspouts with trim paint.

2 Paint the soffit panels and trim with a 4" paint brush. Start by cutting in around the edges of the panels using the narrow edge of the brush, then feather in the broad surfaces of the soffit panels with full loads of paint. Make sure to get good coverage in the groove areas.

TIP: Paint any decorative trim near the top of the house at the same time you paint soffits and fascia. Use a 2½" or 3" paint brush for broader surfaces, and use a sash brush for more intricate trim areas.

(continued next page)

3 Paint the bottom edges of lap siding with the paint brush held flat against the wall. Paint the bottom edges of several siding pieces before returning to paint the faces of the siding boards.

4 Paint the broad faces of the siding boards with a 4" brush. Use the painting technique shown on page 110. Working down from the top, paint only as much surface as you can reach comfortably.

5 Paint all the siding all the way down to the foundation, working from top to bottom. Shift the ladder or scaffolding, and paint the next section. NOTE: Paint up to the edges of end caps and window and door trim that will be painted later. If trim will not be painted, mask it off or use a paint shield.

VARIATION: On board-and-batten or any vertical-panel siding, paint the edges of the battens or top boards first. Paint the faces of the battens before the sides dry, then paint the large, broad surfaces between the battens, feathering in at the edges of the battens. Rollers are good tools for panel siding (use a ⅝"-nap sleeve for rough-textured panels).

VARIATION: On stucco siding, paint the walls with a paint roller and ⅝"-nap sleeve. Use a 3" trim roller or a 3" paint brush for trim.

6 Paint the foundation with anti-chalking masonry primer. Start by cutting in the areas around basement windows. Then, paint the broad surfaces of the foundation with a 4" brush, working the paint into any mortar lines.

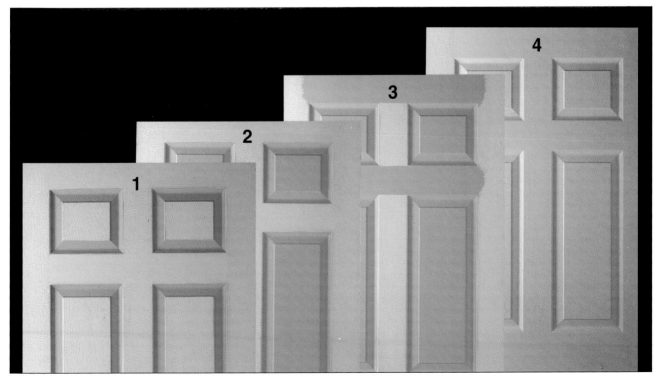

7 Paint doors and windows, using a sash brush. Follow the correct sequence: First, paint the beveled edges of raised door panels, and the insides of muntins or frames on windows; next, paint the faces of the door panels before the edges dry; next, paint rails (horizontal frame members) on doors and windows; last, paint the faces of the stiles (vertical frame members).

(continued next page)

8 Use a trim brush or sash brush and a moderate load of paint to paint the inside edges of door and window jambs, casings, and brick molding. NOTE: The surfaces on the interior side of the door stop usually match the color of the interior trim.

9 Paint the outside edges of casings and brick molding, using a sash brush (mask off freshly painted siding after it has dried).

10 Paint the faces of door jambs, casings, and brick molding, feathering fresh paint around the painted edges.

11 Paint wooden door thresholds and porch floors. Use specially-formulated enamel floor paint for maximum durability.

Index

Cowles Creative Publishing, Inc.
offers a variety of how-to books.
For information write:
Cowles Creative Publishing
Subscriber Books
5900 Green Oak Drive
Minnetonka, MN 55343